Forgiveness

Workbook

Dr. DOUGLAS McDUFFIE

Professor of Psychology

and

Author of

You Can Bounce Back

"The Psychology Of A Preacher In Prison"

Second Printing and Revision

Spring 2013

Copyright 2010 By Dr. Douglas McDuffie

Cheudi Publishing Plano, Texas 75094

Manufactured in the USA 10987654321

Contents

Foreword

Every effort has been made to produce a workbook that covers the subject of the workshop that is informative and factual. Information was taken from the book "Common Sense Parents" by Sue and Henry O. Adkins, additional researched information gathered from Newspaper, periodicals and the internet. All researched sources are cited throughout the workbook.

Privacy Notice

Introduction

Forgive all who have offended you, not for them, but for yourself. *~Harriet Nelson*

It has been said that Forgiveness is a liberating experience. It can bring a sense of relief from the past that one can never anticipate. It can keep one grounded in the present, it can build a better future and help us let go of the past. Many have the misconception that the person for whom the forgiveness is directed is the unfortunate one. On the contrary, the person holding forgiveness in abeyance is the one who is full of negative feelings. The one refusing to forgive is the one who tosses and turns all night unable to sleep. **Forgiveness can be liberating only if we are willing to Forgive.**

NOTES_____

_____

_____

_____

_____

_____

_____

_____

To Give Forgiveness is a Choice

"Forgiveness is not an emotion, it's a decision." -Randall Worley

Like all things in your life, forgiveness is a choice. Many believe that to forgive is doing something for someone else, but rather to forgive is for ourselves not for the other person. A famous philosopher once said, "to forgive is like lifting a heavy weight from one's brain, from one's heart and from one's spirit. When forgiveness is finally given a feeling of relief and satisfaction fills one's entire being. When a person forgives there is suddenly room in one's heart for more positive productive thoughts. Those negative weights manifest themselves in the form of resentment, in the form of mistrust and in the form of no respect but when one forgives resentment no longer exists, trust becomes easier and respect for others becomes common place.

NOTES_____

_____

_____

_____

_____

_____

_____

_____

To Receive Forgiveness Is Also a Choice

Forgiveness is a funny thing. It warms the heart and cools the sting. ~William Arthur Ward

By making the choice to grant forgiveness, you will have brought yourself one step closer to living a life of fulfillment, joy, and deep inner peace. Because you decided to forgive does not automatically insure that the forgiven will gracefully receive that forgiveness. Sometimes when you insist on delivering forgiveness in person it can cause a new problem, especially when one has no knowledge of why they would need or want your forgiveness. Remember to forgive is not generally for the other person, but rather for you. It is different when someone ask for your forgiveness. Then and only then is face-to-face forgiveness appropriate. To receive forgiveness is their choice, your choice is to forgive. Nothing more.

NOTES_____

_____

_____

_____

_____

_____

_____

_____

_____

Forgiveness Does Not Come Easy

It is easier to forgive an enemy than to forgive a friend. ~William Blake

It is not uncommon for Christians to have questions about forgiveness. Forgiveness does not come easy for most of us. Our natural instinct is to recoil in self-protection when we've been injured. We don't naturally overflow with mercy, grace and forgiveness when we've been wronged, we must forgive not for the person that wronged us, but rather for ourselves. When we are unforgiving the results upon our spirit is less than what God would it to be.

NOTES_____

_____

_____

_____

_____

_____

_____

_____

_____

_____

_____

The Consequences of an Unforgiving Spirit

Forgiving seems almost unnatural. Our sense of fairness tells us people should pay for the wrong they do. But forgiving is love's power to break nature's rule. ~Lewis B. Smedes

The unforgiving person harbors feelings of resentment, anger, hurt, or envy, which can have serious physical and emotional consequences. The unforgiving person becomes unable to allow feelings of love to emanate and instead their health is compromised. In order to restore and maintain good mental and emotional health, the unforgiving person must learn how to **forgive**.

NOTES_____

_____

_____

_____

_____

_____

_____

_____

_____

_____

_____

"When you hold resentment toward another, you are bound to that person or condition by an emotional link that is stronger than steel. Forgiveness is the only way to dissolve that link and get free." -Catherine Ponder

Recent studies have clearly indicated that anger and resentment doubled the risk of heart attacks in women with previous coronary problems. There have been other studies that revealed that many fatal diseases such as cancer are also caused by anger and resentment. Feelings of resentment is an unnatural function. So when you continuously harbor these feelings it can take the form of physical stress. When the body holds anger and resentment, the stress response is triggered. Heart rate increases, blood pressure increases, muscles tense, jaws clench, and tension builds. The result is chronic pain and headaches, restricted blood flow to certain areas of the body, reduced oxygen supply to the cells in the body, and diminished healing. As the resentment lingers, blood flow to the heart is compromised. The breathing is affected, the immune system functions at an impaired level, leaving you vulnerable to infections.

NOTES_____

_____

_____

_____

_____

_____

_____

"Anger makes you smaller, while forgiveness forces you to grow beyond what you were." -Cherie Carter-Scott

Besides your physical health, your emotional and mental health is also compromised when you are unable to forgive. You become easily distracted and lose focus. You experienced decreased productivity and this sets in more frustration. Your anger and frustration injects more negativity into your psyche, which gets transferred to all other areas of your life. You become impatient, and difficult to deal with. Before long, you are impossible to be around. Holding grudges is a negative emotion. The more negativity the mind cherishes, the more it festers and spreads, affecting your disposition and behaviors. If negativity is what you put out, that's exactly what will come back to you. Allow more positive flow of emotion in your life. Learn to let go of the negative emotions.

NOTES_____

_____

_____

_____

_____

_____

_____

_____

_____

_____

Forgiveness is almost a selfish act because of its immense benefits to the one who forgives." -Lawana Blackwell

Examine your life. Are you an unforgiving person? Do you have a tendency to hold on to old feelings of **resentment** and **anger**? If so, begin today to search for the true you again. You cannot even imagine how it feels to forgive and release these mental tensions. Focus on what is truly important to you and don't get stuck in a world of **unforgiveness**. Look for ways to open your inner self allowing more freedom within. Allow your vitality to improve. Begin to enjoy good health and a harmonious life again. Begin to **forgive** - life is too short to hold grudges.

NOTES_____

_____

_____

_____

_____

_____

_____

_____

_____

_____

Forgive To Heal

Never does the human soul appear so strong as when it forgoes revenge, and dares forgive an injury. ~E.H. Chapin

Someone once said that when you don't forgive it is like taking poison and waiting for the other person to die. When you don't forgive the only person that suffer is you. When you withhold forgiveness, you withhold a piece of your soul. Unless you forgive those that inflicted the hurt, you cannot heal and you will continue to hurt until you do. But, understand even when you forgive the pain does not go away immediately, it's what you do with that pain. Don't lock it in. Let it go. When you let it go your life gets better. Your life becomes easier and a measure of happiness returns. You will begin to heal only when you forgive. Forgiveness is not a cure all, but it does help.

NOTES_____

_____

_____

_____

_____

_____

_____

The results of an unforgiving spirit

Forgiveness is the fragrance the violet sheds on the heel that has crushed it.
~Mark Twain

(1) The ability to forgive is a mental, emotional, physical and spiritual process.

(2) The process of forgiving releases resentment, anger and ill feelings one has toward another person.

(3) Forgiveness is mental. You have to make a conscious decision to let go of resentments.

(4) It is emotional because feelings of anger and resentment are strong emotions that must be released.

(5) It is physical because the unforgiving person can experience many physical symptoms that can develop into more serious physical conditions.

(6) It is also spiritual because you must feel inspired to let go and to pardon but once you do so the soul is cleansed and liberated.

NOTES_____

_____

_____

_____

_____

_____

_____

The difficulty with Forgiveness

The weak can never forgive. Forgiveness is the attribute of the strong. ~Mahatma Gandhi.

The difficulty with Forgiveness is that the <u>unconscious</u> mind is struggling with the <u>conscious</u> mind which may have caused wounds inflicted by one person upon another. In Sigmund Freud's psychoanalytic theory of personality, the conscious mind includes everything that is inside of our awareness. This is the aspect of our mental processing that we can think and talk about in a rational way. The conscious mind includes such things as the sensations, perceptions, memories, feeling and fantasies inside of our current awareness. Closely allied with the conscious mind is the pre-conscious, which includes the things that we are not thinking of at the moment but which we can easily draw into conscious awareness.

NOTES_____

_____

_____

_____

_____

_____

_____

_____

We Forgive By Faith

And I am certain that God, who began the good work within you, will continue his work until it is finally finished on the day when Christ Jesus returns. Philippians 1:6 (NLT)

We forgive **by faith**, out of obedience. Since forgiveness goes against our nature, we must forgive by faith, whether we feel like it or not. We must trust God to do the work in us that needs to be done so that the forgiveness will be complete. I believe God honors our commitment to obey Him and our desire to please him when we choose to forgive. He completes the work in his time. We must continue to forgive (our job), by faith, until the work of forgiveness (the Lord's job), is done in our hearts.

NOTES_____

_____

_____

_____

_____

_____

_____

_____

_____

_____

_____

The Psychological and Spiritual Aspects of Forgiveness

Forgiving is love's toughest work, and love's biggest risk. ...unknown

We should examine forgiveness from the aspect of the Psychological and the Spiritual because God has created us as physical, social, mental, emotional and spiritual being. Psychological forgiveness involves the affective, cognitive and behavioral systems (how the person forgiving feels, thinks, and behaves). The psychological response that is forgiveness includes the absence of negative effects, and judgment, but instead includes the presence of positive affects, judgment and behavior. Psychological forgiveness is a powerful therapeutic intervention and as an intellectual exercise in which the patient makes a decision to forgive. It becomes a voluntary act and a decision as well as a choice about how one deals with the past. In other words, one must let go of all recorded wrongs, the need for vengeance and one must release all negative feelings of bitterness and resentment.

NOTES_____

_____

_____

_____

_____

_____

"If you haven't forgiven yourself something, how can you forgive others?"
...Dolores Huerta

The goal is to have mastery over a hurt or a wound and the process through which an injured person first fights off, then embraces, and at last conquers a situation that nearly destroys. It becomes an intra-psychic interpersonal way of giving up one's right to hurt back. Psychological Trends focus on the benefits of forgiveness for the **forgiver** in the therapeutic and healing process. Base of this psychological perspective the experience of forgiveness is now **spiritual**. Psychological Perspective acknowledges that forgiveness is transpersonal as well Interpersonal because forgiveness has qualities that transcend one's relationship with the person being forgiven and opens the forgiver to the world in entirely new ways. It has more than a purely interpersonal quality, the difference from the psychological aspect and spiritual aspect- qualities of gift/grace, because forgiveness involves interpersonal and the divine – they are inextricably related, therefore one cannot consider the forgiveness of another outside the context of God.

NOTES_____

_____

_____

_____

_____

_____

_____

_____

Be kind to one another, tenderhearted, forgiving one another, as God in Christ forgave you. ...Ephesians 4:32 (NIV)

While psychological perspective would have us to believe that forgiveness is "just a happy trait of character or an acquired psychological disposition." For a Christian the very altitude/root of forgiving is the core of experience, the utter forgiveness of God in their lives. In other words every experience of forgiveness has **God** as its ultimate point of beginning.

NOTES_____

_____

_____

_____

_____

_____

_____

_____

_____

_____

_____

_____

_____

_____

Forgiveness Is Unconditional

Forgiveness does not change the past, but it does enlarge the future. ~Paul Boese

Don't make change a pre-requisite to forgiveness. Your forgiveness must be unconditional with no strings attached. The person that committed the hurtful act against you may or may not change. To insist that they do before you forgive them insures that they will not. When you threaten or bully someone by telling them you will never forgive unless they change, usually will give them a reason not to change. Just forgive and do not worry about what the other person does. Your job is to forgive not to force change. Let them make their changes (if indeed they do) in their own time and in their own way. Their change is not your business or your responsibility. It solely belongs to them. Your responsibility is to forgive and to forgive unconditionally.

NOTES_____

_____

_____

_____

_____

_____

_____

_____

_____

The Best Reason to Forgive

For if you forgive men when they sin against you, your heavenly Father will also forgive you. But if you do not forgive men their sins, your Father will not forgive your sins. Matthew 6:14-16 <u>(NIV)</u>

The best reason to forgive is because Jesus commanded us to forgive. We learn from Scripture, if we don't forgive, neither will we be forgiven.

NOTES_____

_____

_____

_____

_____

_____

_____

_____

_____

_____

_____

_____

_____

Pray For The Person We Need To Forgive

Do not judge, and you will not be judged. Do not condemn, and you will not be condemned. Forgive, and you will be forgiven. Luke 6:37 (NIV)

We must pray for the person we need to forgive. We can pray for God to deal with the injustices, for God to judge the person's life, and then we can leave that prayer at the altar. We no longer have to carry the anger. Although it is normal for us to feel anger toward sin and injustice, it is not our job to judge the other person in their sin.

NOTES_____

_____

_____

_____

_____

_____

_____

_____

_____

_____

_____

_____

_____

_____

Forgiveness Is Only Completed When We Experience Freedom

Corrie T. Boom, a Christian woman who survived a Nazi concentration camp during the Holocaust, said, "Forgiveness is to set a prisoner free, and to realize the prisoner was you."

We will know the work of forgiveness is complete when we experience the freedom that comes as a result. We are the ones who suffer most when we choose not to forgive. When we do forgive, the Lord sets our hearts free from the <u>anger</u>, <u>bitterness</u>, <u>resentment</u> and <u>hurt</u> that previously imprisoned us.

He who cannot forgive breaks the bridge over which he himself must pass.
~George Herbert

NOTES_____

_____

_____

_____

_____

_____

_____

_____

_____

_____

_____

Forgive and Forget

I can forgive, but I cannot forget, is only another way of saying, I will not forgive.
Henry Ward Beecher

If you can't forgive and forget, you have not forgiven. ~Robert Brault

Many believe that it is okay to forgive and not forget. We've heard people say, "I have forgiven but I will never forget." Studies have shown that individuals that say they have forgiven but will not forget have not forgiven and have no intention of forgiving. Whatever hurt one encountered remains fresh in their memory when there is a refusal to forget. Forget in this sense simply means to put aside or leave in the past, not to re-visit (ever). When one purposely keeps a past hurtful situation alive in their memory forgiveness cannot come forth and given. When an unpleasant memory is kept alive it is difficult if not impossible to make better ones that will lead to a happy fulfilling life. Therefore, forgiveness has not been given if one cannot forget.

NOTES_____

_____

_____

_____

_____

_____

NOTES

Appendix

Suggested Reading

The Art of Forgiving : When You Need to Forgive and Don't Know How by Lewis Smedes

Forgive and Forget : Healing the Hurts We Don't Deserve by Lewis B. Smedes

Forgiveness : How to Make Peace With Your Past and Get on With Your Life by Sidney B. Simon, Suzanne Simon

The Unburdened Heart: 5 Keys to Forgiveness and Freedom by Mariah Burton Nelson

The Power of Apology by Beverly Engel

Forgive For Good by Frederic Luskin

How Can I Forgive You? By Janis A. Spring

Forgive and Love Again by John Nieder

Forgive Me by Amanda Eyre Ward

How To Forgive by John Monbourquette

How to Forgive When You Can't Forget by Charles Klein

Why Forgive by Johann Christoph

If I Can Forgive, So Can You by Denise Linn

To Order additional Copies of this workbook, please use this order form:

Name: _____

Address: _____

City: _____   State /Prov: _____

Zip / Postal Code: _____Telephone(s): _____

_____copies @ $15.00 US / $20.00 Cdn: $_____

Shipping: ($5.00 first book - $1.50 each additional book) $_____

Texas residents add 8.25% tax $_____Total amount enclosed

Mail to: You Can Bounce Back, Cheudi Publishing, P. O. Box 940572-0572, Plano, Texas 75094

Workshops and Workbooks

By

Dr. Douglas McDuffie

You Can Bounce Back

Successfully Adjusting To Prison

Coming Home (from Prison)

Everything Women Need To Know About Men Coming Home from Prison

About The Author

Douglas McDuffie, Counselor

Douglas McDuffie is a minister who lectures and presents workshops across the country. He has a Bachelor of Arts degree from Hiram College, a Master of Arts degree in Counseling from Amberton University, Dallas, Texas; a Masters and a Doctorate in Ministry from Slidell Theological Seminary and is a Certified Family Development Specialist from the University of Iowa School of Social Work.

Cheudi Publishing

Plano, Texas 75094

www.ingramcontent.com/pod-product-compliance
Lightning Source LLC
Chambersburg PA
CBHW081159090426
42736CB00017B/3392

* 9 7 8 0 9 8 4 6 0 8 3 6 2 *